REAL
ESTATE

REAL ESTATE
Rules!

52 ways to achieve success in real estate

written by **DEBBI DiMAGGIO**

illustrated by **STEVE HICKNER**

BRIGANTINE MEDIA

Illustrations by Steve Hickner

Brigantine Media
211 North Avenue, St. Johnsbury, Vermont 05819
Phone: 802-751-8802 | Fax: 802-751-8804
Email: neil@brigantinemedia.com
Website: www.brigantinemedia.com

ISBN 978-1-9384065-4-6

Dedication

To my husband and soulmate, Adam Betta,
to whom I couldn't soar without.

Acknowledgments

It must be noted that anyone I meet usually moves from acquaintance to friend within moments of meeting. Certainly, for the people mentioned here, the word "friend" precedes their professional titles.

To author, songwriter, and business consultant Gini Graham Scott of Changemakers Productions, who encouraged me to write a second real estate book after reading *The Art of Real Estate* and put me in touch with many wonderful publishers. To friend and business manager Angela Psuik, who is always looking out for my best interests. To my publicist, Liz Kelly, who has been instrumental in sharing *The Art of Real Estate* and *Contained Beauty* with the public through television, radio, social media, and print, while articulating and fine-tuning Debbi DiMaggio, the brand. To both publicists Liz Kelly and Doris Bergman for inviting me to the party—the Doris Bergman Gift Lounge during Emmy and Oscar weeks—what a unique experience! To my parents, Vince and Midge DiMaggio, my loving husband, Adam Betta, my precious children, Bianca and Chase, my Aunt Renee DiMaggio, my mother-in law, Carolyn Betta, my sister-in-law, Gigi Betta, my brother, Michael DiMaggio, sister-in-law, Lisa DiMaggio, nephew, Cole, and niece, Ali DiMaggio, whom we all refer to as "Mini Me." Without family we have no one to share our ups and our downs and to celebrate life with, as loud as it may get in our very Sicilian-Italian family, always accompanied with hands waving and elevated voices.

And of course, to my hard- and fast-working editor, Janis Raye, and publisher, Neil Raphel of Brigantine Media, and my fabulous illustrator, Steve Hickner. Teamwork at its finest!

The Rules

PART ONE: SELLING YOURSELF

1 Become a personality.   3
2 Exceed expectations.   5
3 Put your name on the bottom line.   7
4 Channel your inner Tom Hanks.   9
5 Trust other agents.   11
6 Be careful what you say.   13
7 Google yourself!   15
8 Toot your own horn.   17
9 Take some time off.   19
10 Act like you mean business.   21
11 Keep up with the Kardashians!   22

PART TWO: MARKETING PROPERTIES

12 Educate your sellers.   27
13 Sell a little harder in a buyer's market.   30
14 Stage it.   33
15 Make a great first impression.   36
16 Take charge of the makeover.   39
17 Create property-specific websites.   41
18 Don't skip the print.   43
19 Use a professional photographer.   45
20 Try a sketch.   47
21 Send postcards.   49
22 Treat luxury properties differently.   51
23 Write a love letter.   53
24 Tell the seller to take a hike.   55

The Rules

PART THREE: WORKING WITH CLIENTS

25 Be the captain of the ship.   59

26 Fill out your real estate checklist.   61

27 Be like Jeeves.   63

28 Convince sellers to reject being a FSBO   65
(For Sale by Owner).

29 Don't rely on online services for pricing.   67

30 Be conservative when pricing a home.   69

31 Stay firm on your commission.   71

32 Don't take it personally.   73

33 Pre-prepare an offer.   75

34 Put the right offer on the table.   77

35 Close the deal.   79

36 Be on time.   81

PART FOUR: BUILDING YOUR BUSINESS

37 Form your dream team.   85

38 Avoid the four biggest mistakes new agents make.   87

39 Choose the right real estate firm.   90

40 Learn how to negotiate.   92

41 Specialize.   95

42 Hit a "home" run.   97

43 Embrace the Internet.   100

44 Look for leads in unlikely places.   102

45 Plant, water, and grow your relationships.   105

46 Learn to love floor duty.   108

47 Solicit testimonials.   110

48 Set out the welcome mat.   112

49 Structure your time.   114

50 Be a busy (and smart) bee.   117

51 Widen your "sphere of influence."   119

52 Throw a party!   122

CONCLUSION   124

PART ONE

Selling Yourself

Become a personality.

MY NAME IS Debbi DiMaggio.

I'm a real estate professional, author, and speaker. I'm also a devoted mother and wife.

I'm involved in philanthropy and charities. My role model is Lady Diana. She was a global ambassador for charitable causes, and a woman with her own sense of style who could rise above the constant drama in her life.

My business mission is to empower real estate agents to be the best they can be. I offer advice to agents on my website, blogs, through LinkedIn, and through speeches around the country.

This book is part of my business identity.

I've tried to create a personality that is unique. You should, too.

When you're selling real estate, you're selling yourself—your strengths, your reputation, your expertise, and your personality.

Your business identity is going to be different than mine. You have your own distinctive characteristics to promote.

You are in charge. Create your persona.

Be a star!

Exceed expectations.

MY MOTTO IS "Do whatever it takes to help your clients and sell their homes with ease and grace." In my real estate practice, I try to live up to that pledge. Here are some of the things I've done for clients:

- Hauled personal items to the trash for the client who simply left it behind.

- Took a client's donation items to the Salvation Army.

- Babysat a client's child when the client went out of town for a long weekend.

- Hosted a client for one week at our home until their home was available to move into.

I'm not suggesting you have to do any of these items, and (if you're lucky) they may not come up as part of your transactions.

But whenever possible, try to exceed the expectations of your clients. I think it's the main reason I've achieved success in real estate, and I think it will work for you, too.

Put your name on the bottom line.

OSCAR GUERRERO WAS a salesman at a car dealership. A friend of mine went to Oscar to buy a car, but he checked the same car's prices at another dealership.

"Oscar," my friend said, "here's your offer for the car and here's the competing offer from another car company. The offers are for the same car and I'd like to use you, but you are $300 more than your competitor. I'm sorry, but I'm going to use the competitor."

Oscar said, "You're missing the difference between the two offers. My name's on the bottom line of our contract. And that will make all the difference."

Oscar explained that if my friend ever needed service, he'd personally pick up the car and bring it back. If my friend had a problem with the car, he could call Oscar day or night, and Oscar would take care of it. Sure, my friend would be paying a little more money, but wasn't it worth it?

Of course, my friend bought the car from Oscar.

Putting your name on the bottom line says that you are committing to your clients. In the real estate world, that means giving out your phone number so your client can reach you whenever it's necessary. It means quality marketing, open houses, and clear communication. It means working your hardest to achieve your client's goals.

Put your name on the bottom line when a client lists with you. Let clients know that *you* are part of the contract.

Channel your inner Tom Hanks.

JUSTIN BIEBER'S ANTICS may be fun to watch, but when clients are buying or selling a home, they want a real estate agent who's like Tom Hanks.

Everybody likes Tom Hanks. Who wouldn't want to do business with him? He seems like the nicest, most reputable guy in the world. He played the widowed dad every woman wanted to marry in *Sleepless in Seattle*, the clearheaded astronaut Jim Lovell in *Apollo 13*, and Sheriff Woody in *Toy Story*. He's today's version of Gary Cooper and Jimmy Stewart.

Be more like Tom Hanks!

Be polite. Even if a client is annoying, be on your best behavior. If need be, bite your tongue.

Be interested in your client. Spend time talking with your client about what he wants in a home, about the needs of his family, activities he enjoys, if schools are important, if he wants to be near amenities such as shops, boutiques, restaurants, and cultural centers. Get to know what's important to your client so you don't waste his time and yours looking at properties that aren't suitable.

Be upbeat. Never cast aspersions on other agents, homes, or neighborhoods. Let your client make up his or her own mind. Your job is to find the best home, not to run down people or places.

Be on time. I can't imagine that Tom Hanks keeps people waiting!

Act like Tom Hanks (I know, nobody can act like Tom Hanks). You won't win an Oscar, but you'll win the respect of others.

RULE
5

Trust other agents.

I TREAT OTHER agents with utmost respect, and expect other agents to trust me and treat me with that same respect in return. I like to think of all other agents as partners and colleagues, not as competitors.

Here's why: the most important factor in any real estate transaction is trust. I trust other agents to give me honest information. And I do the same with them. If there is a problem with a listing (a leaky roof, a title concern), I disclose it right away. When you know what you are dealing with it's a lot easier to resolve a tricky situation. When someone is hiding a defect, eventually you'll find out about it and that can lead to distrust, if not a lawsuit.

I am not naive. I know that some people are greedy and are not pleasant to work with. But I'm a firm believer in treating people with respect and trust until I find out that they are trying to deceive me. Then I react strongly and make sure the situation is fixed. If it happens again, I will try to avoid dealing with that particular agent again. Of course, that's not always easy if the agent has a property your client is interested in. But she will not receive any favors from me, and probably not from many others if her reputation precedes her. If you are known as a trustworthy agent, your colleagues in the real estate community will often choose to work with you instead of another agent who has a bad reputation.

Start with trust. You can build a great relationship that way.

Be careful what you say.

WORDS ARE POWERFUL. Words can hurt. Some words are a code violation. And as a real estate agent, you have to be especially careful that you don't inadvertently offend the buyer or seller, or incur a HUD violation.

When you are dealing with a home sale, even the most common words sometimes have connotations you want to avoid. So be careful!

For example, consider this list of words that can cause problems.

Walk. What? Why? Well, not everyone can walk. And while the term "walk-up" is not a Fair Housing violation, you'd be better off not using it.

Family room. Be careful. Everyone doesn't have a family. What is or who makes up a family, exactly? Use "rumpus room" or "media room" instead.

Master bedroom. Can be taken as sexist. I know that most people are comfortable with this term. But would it hurt to say "primary bedroom" or "largest bedroom" as a substitute?

Safe, secure neighborhood. You probably don't know if there has been a crime or problem on this street. Better avoid that phrase. Better yet, have your client check with the local police department.

His and hers. Try not to use gender-specific labels.

Each region of the country has its own potentially sensitive terms. Avoid the words that can hurt people in your community, particularly words that refer to the race or nationality of community members. Check the Fair Housing Act to be sure. Don't speak or communicate in any way (such as texting or e-mailing) without considering if your words could have unintended consequences.

Google yourself!

THE FIRST THING a client or potential client will do to find out more information about you is to Google your name. If the first three hits are photos of you drinking at wild parties, clients may be reluctant to trust you with the sale of their precious home.

Google yourself. Find out what the Internet says about you.

Be careful about the images and messages you post on social media and what you send out in e-mails. Whatever privacy protections you choose, there is always the chance that one of your crazy pictures will make its way across the Internet.

Treat all your online correspondence as public. If the government isn't watching you, you can be sure that your friends and future clients are.

But on the flip side: In order to gain business and develop your branding, you need to be found online. Be sure your social media and websites provide accurate phone numbers and other contact information. Make sure you publicize your bio. If you want to stand out in the crowded real estate field, develop your online presence—not just real estate-related posts, but a bit about your real life and personality. If you are an avid tennis player or enjoy cooking or golf, share that with your audience. Clients like to bond with people. Allow them to bond with you!

So Google yourself. I'm sure your clients will be doing it, too!

Toot your own horn.

YOU KNOW YOU'RE good. So don't be shy about telling the world. Potential clients may not be aware of your accomplishments and ability to transact real estate.

Create your bio for your website, social media platforms, and print material. The bio should point out your strongest points, including real estate specialties and educational achievements (when appropriate). If you have lots of experience, include how long you've been in real estate. If you're a new agent, maybe you can talk about how well you know the local area. Be sure to mention the kinds of work you do to get the best results for your clients.

If you have achieved success as a real estate agent, be sure to tout it in your advertising. A phrase such as "Top 1% (or 5% or 10%) Real Estate Agent in the US" helps gain customer confidence.

Toot your own horn. Loudly. You don't have to be Donald Trump, but you need to get the word out.

Take some time off.

YOUR LIFE AS a real estate agent is often nonstop. You are running from appointment to appointment, and squeezing in floor duty. You are busy acquiring new listings and trying to sell the listings you already have. Everyone you meet is a client or potential client, as you are always on stage. Who knows where the next million-dollar lead will come from? And, of course, you have to squeeze out time every day to reach out to the world on social media.

Whew!

It seems as if you will never leave this treadmill. But you have to!

People are most productive when they give themselves a chance to refresh, reorganize and reboot.

Take time out each day to relax. It could be taking a walk around the block, doing a crossword puzzle, reading a novel, or even meditating—whatever gets you out of the daily hassles of being a real estate agent. Your mind needs a diversion from time to time. When you relax, you pave the way for a more energized you.

Take a day off every now and then. Life insurance salesman Sid Friedman was one of the most successful life insurance agents in the country. But every once in a while he would take a whole day off to play golf or listen to music or just watch TV. He said that the time off made him far more productive the rest of the week.

Take a long weekend every now and then throughout the year. We find even 24 hours away allows us to renew. Midweek is often the perfect time to escape before the hectic Sunday Open House schedule begins. Travel. Relax. Renew. See some new sights and gain a new perspective. Get someone to cover for you and don't even think about the work (if that's possible!). You'll come back refreshed, and your family life will benefit. Believe it or not, life at the office and your clients will go on without you. You need the time off so you can be a more productive agent.

Relax.

Refresh.

Repeat.

Act like you mean business.

BEING A REAL estate agent is very much like being an actor. If you don't like the limelight, you are in the wrong business.

Like a Broadway entertainer, you have to please a roomful of people. You are being watched and listened to constantly. How you greet and interact with potential buyers, sellers, looky-loos, and even neighbors will determine your success.

Relish the spotlight. Psyche yourself up when you are holding an open house or a private showing. This is your time to delight the audience. What you wear, how you talk, your enthusiasm, your honesty, your insights will all be judged by your audience. Be ready for the show.

There's no business like show business—except, maybe, the real estate business!

Keep up with the Kardashians!

THE KARDASHIANS MAY not be your cup of tea, but boy, are they successful! From a sex video to weddings and a gender transformation, they have provided people with fascinating entertainment while building a media empire that churns out greenbacks.

While you may not want to emulate the Kardashians' personal lives, you might want to learn from and emulate some of their marketing strategies.

Here are some tips from the profitable world of the Kardashians:

- **Take advantage of social media**: The Kardashians are in your face every day. And most of their hijinks are highly visual. It's a visual world these days, so be sure you're posting pictures all the time. Photographs of your properties tell your story faster than thousands of words. Just as Kim Kardashian West says, "As long as they are talking about me, I am relevant."

- **Make it interesting:** The Kardashians are always coming up with another interesting wrinkle in their lives. You have to make selling real estate interesting. How about using drones to give exciting video views of your listings? You have to be in front of your competition if you're going to make a splash.

- **Use people in pictures:** Make sure your faces and your clients' faces appear in your advertising. Clients relate to people. You are not only selling a home, you are selling a dream. Kim Kardashian West's latest book, *Selfish*, a book of selfies, is a big hit. Follow Kim. Use the power of faces in your advertising.

People are fascinated by the lifestyles of the rich and famous. Try to capture some of that magic in your advertising.

PART TWO

Marketing Properties

Educate your sellers.

MOST REAL ESTATE agents concentrate on getting the deal. They meet with potential sellers and concentrate on getting the sellers to sign a listing agreement.

That's all well and good. If you don't sign a seller up quickly, you are in danger of losing the listing.

But in your initial meeting with the seller, you must educate as well as sell. Most people buy and sell only two or three homes in their lifetime. They aren't experts—you are. It may have been 20 or 30 years since they last bought or sold a home. Help them in that very first meeting by offering plenty of information about how the process will work.

I prefer to educate rather than sell. I thoroughly review the process with a potential client. If we are compatible and they like what I am sharing, then we are a match—no selling involved. If we aren't a match, we aren't a match, and no amount of knowledge or skill will change that.

Discuss how you will assist them in getting their home ready for a sale. If they need it, you'll book the contractors and inspectors to help them put the home's best foot forward.

Explain to them what works best to make the sale process go as smoothly as possible. This includes having the home available for showings whenever it is convenient for the buyers, while the seller must vacate the premises, giving the buyer privacy to preview their home alone.

Explain the sales process—the forms the seller will sign, what inspections will be needed, and what the closing will be like. Make sure the seller is aware that nothing is settled until both buyer(s) and seller(s) have signed the closing papers, the lender has funded the loan, the buyer's funds are in and have cleared the bank, and lastly, the recording has taken place at the county recorder's office. And that you are responsible for making sure all those things occur.

I package my selling tips into a "success sheet" for sellers. It's a valuable resource that I give to sellers at our first meeting, which often helps seal the deal for the listing. Providing clarity in a very complicated process is what a seller appreciates most.

Post these tips on your website, too. Use them

to generate future business from people who may be checking your website. Many agents are afraid that their competitors might steal their best tips, but having an informative website is more important than worrying about your competitors. The more you stay ahead of the real estate game, the harder your competitors will have to work to catch up!

Sell a little harder in a buyer's market.

THERE IS A tremendous difference in selling real estate in a hot market and one where there is a dearth of buyers.

How great is it to be a real estate agent in a seller's market? You put your home up for sale, run an open house, and the offers start pouring in. A full price offer. Another offer that is ten percent above list price. An amazing offer that is twenty percent above list price!

Wow! That was fun!

Hot real estate markets shift over time. Consider the plight of the real estate agent in a buyer's market. There are so many homes for sale, and there are not many being sold. A property can be on the market for two, three, or four years (yes, *years*, not months) with very few showings. The local industry may be struggling, crime may be on the rise, there may not be much in the way of amenities in the town.

What's a real estate agent in that town to do?

Plenty! Real estate is cyclical, so it's important to learn how to sell real estate in any market. Here are my tips:

- Price the home right—not necessarily at the price the seller wants. Show your sellers why the offer price you recommend is the one to use to market the home. Do your research and then give them the area comps so they understand what the current values are. Homes that aren't priced right will sit forever. (Even in a seller's market!)

- Educate your sellers. The price they paid for the home when they bought it is no longer relevant. And what their neighbors got for the home next door six months ago may not be what buyers are willing to pay today. That buyer might have overpaid. Comparables aren't always comparable.

- Make your home "turnkey," not a turkey. Be sure the home sparkles and all the repair work needed is complete. This is no time for a stain on the carpet or a broken light fixture!

- Offer incentives. Think out of the box. What about offering an incentive to the buyer's agent, maybe an extra percentage of commission? How about a bonus to the buyer's agent for making a sale on a high-priced property? I have offered a week at my timeshare as an incentive for an agent to find a buyer, and it has brought results. Make your home stand out from all the other offerings.

If your real estate market isn't up to par, you have to be even better at what you do. Somebody will make money selling real estate in your market. Why not you?

Stage it.

I'VE BET YOU'VE heard that homes look better if they are just white walls and bare floors.

Forget it!

Most buyers lack one essential to appreciate a home: imagination. An empty home looks simply... empty. And a cluttered home with personal details is too hard for most buyers to envision as the home they would want to live in.

I advise agents to stage every home they market. I have found it crucial for making a sale for the maximum price. You don't have to hire a professional staging firm, although that may be important for the higher-priced homes. For some homes, you and the sellers can stage it using their belongings and a few of your own. But in our market and in most cases,

I highly recommend using a professional stager or (what has become a new business) a stager who will edit the owner's home and stage using some of the owner's belongings while bringing in a few accent pieces. This is less costly than a full staging job and can be very effective. It is much better than leaving the staging up to the seller. It's just not what they do or know. Never forget that you are the professional and they are relying on your expertise. Don't short-change your reputation or your client.

Here's how the staging experts from HGTV suggest ways a seller can stage her own home:

- Get rid of clutter! The less junk the better. Remove family photographs, children's toys, and excess furniture. Make it look like a model home, not like someone really lives there. Professional stagers take away as much as half the home's furnishings (although we prefer a vacant home prior to staging) to make every room look larger. Your seller may not be able to do that, but have him consider every piece of furniture and put into storage everything that isn't absolutely necessary.

- Then reposition the remaining furniture into conversational groupings. Move pieces around the home to find where a chair or table works best.

- Make sure every room has a purpose. If there's one room that collects junk (and we all have one of these!), put the junk in storage, then add a cozy chair, a book-filled shelving unit, and a reading lamp, and voila! It's a library space.

- Brighten the lights. Change out bulbs to the highest wattage you can use. Homes that are dark don't show as well. A simple fix like replacing light bulbs goes a long way.

- Don't forget to have the home cleaned by a professional and the windows washed inside and out. No one wants to see spider webs and scuff marks when they're touring a home.

- Make sure all the lawns and gardens are in great shape. Trim bushes, remove large trees that cover the home, reseed the front lawn if necessary, plant some annual flowers, and lay mulch. Curb appeal is not a myth!

The staging a seller does can make the difference between a home that lingers on the market and one that sells for top dollar.

Make a great first impression.

WE'VE TALKED ABOUT the need to stage a home to give it that designer-home anonymity so your seller will get the highest offer possible (Rule 14). But there's more to do to get a home ready for sale.

You want every home to create a great first impression. Help your seller understand what kind of work needs to be done before the home starts to be shown to potential buyers.

- Repair: Are there repairs that the homeowner has been meaning to make for years? The cracked concrete in the front walk, the missing closet door handle, the leaking bathroom faucet. Most people live with some imperfections in their home. But potential buyers will zero in on small repairs needed and assume they are indicative of a home that hasn't been well cared for. Repair them before putting the home on the market.

- Repaint: Most homes need a new paint job, inside and out. There's a stain on the ceiling from an old water leak. Paint is peeling from the trim on the south side of the home that gets direct sunlight. Whenever possible, repaint the interior with a neutral palette. Ask the stager to recommend current colors that are in today's taste. For the exterior, I prefer a taupe gray shade that complements the greenery of the garden.

- Deep clean: Carpets must be cleaned, floors scrubbed and buffed, windows washed inside and out, kitchen cabinets and walls grease-free. This kind of cleaning is not the same as everyday tidying—it's probably best to bring in a professional.

- Check appliances: Be sure that all the major appliances are working properly. If not, fix or replace them. Most buyers don't want to have the additional expense of purchasing new appliances when they have just bought a new home. And don't forget to install smoke and carbon monoxide detectors throughout the home.

- Garden: The front lawn must be trimmed and meticulous. A garden that's overgrown makes buyers think about all that work they'll have to do out there—which is not what most people want! Keep up with the garden chores until the home is sold.

You get one chance to make a good first impression. Most buyers will make up their mind right away if the home feels right for them or not. Don't give them any reason to rule out your listings!

Take charge of the makeover.

IN ORDER TO sell a property, the seller has to position the property in the best possible light. When I represent a seller, part of my service is to coordinate, execute, and manage the mini-makeover of the seller's home prior to market.

I prepare a checklist for the makeover that outlines our responsibilities. I ask the sellers to sign the list to be sure everyone is clear.

My makeover checklist:

- The agent will obtain bids for work needed prior to market and inspection reports for the listing.

- The seller will make final decisions on the work to be performed on the property prior to market.

- The seller will negotiate bids with service providers directly.

- The seller will make prompt payments to service providers.

I meet with the service providers and contractors to discuss what I have recommended, but the seller is solely responsible for all payments. I book appointments with the seller at each stage of the improvements to discuss any changes to the plan and witness the progress of the improvements.

When I am closely involved with the mini-makeover, everybody is well informed about the process. I manage expectations and make sure the process goes smoothly.

From Kevin Costner's movie, *Field of Dreams*, "If you build it, they will come." It is so true. If the sellers make the financial investment, they will reap the rewards. A well-run mini-makeover is often the key to selling a property promptly and at the best possible price.

Create property-specific websites.

ALL REAL ESTATE agents work for an agency that has a website (I hope so!).

Many agents have their own personal websites (I hope that's you!). A personal website lets you control your own brand image. It can be a gateway to your Facebook page as well as a link to your agency's website. It is imperative to have your own personal website in order to separate you from the rest. Your website is a place to showcase all you do and have done. Include a list of resources, charity work you might be involved with, your active, pending, and sold listings, along with a plethora of other information. Take a look at www.DiMaggioAndBetta.com to see how I use my website.

But I would take it one step further. For all my listings, I construct a website for each individual listing.

For the Internet address, I use an address-specific web address, such as www.123MainStreet.com.

It can be very inexpensive to set up a website for a property. There are many do-it-yourself sites such as TourFactory, Weebly, and SquareSpace where you can create a powerful website yourself. It's easy to choose a template, add photos, videos and text. The sites look great and the cost is next to nothing.

I believe having personalized websites for your best listings will become quite common in the future. They make it easy for buyers and sellers to preview the most important features of a property. No need to scroll through the MLS—just tell your clients, "Click on 123MainStreet.com." And be sure to share that site throughout all of your social media platforms before it comes to market, to advertise your broker tour, the Sunday Open House and to remind the public of the next open house or to simply alert people that the property is still available.

So get on the bandwagon early. Create personalized sites to grow your business. An added bonus: your clients will be impressed with your out-of-the-ordinary marketing efforts.

RULE
18

Don't skip the print.

IT'S TEMPTING TO put all your resources into the Internet.

In fact, I would recommend putting at least 60 percent of your advertising dollars into online advertising. Online advertising includes your website development, social media advertising, advertising on national real estate sites, and advertising on other local sites where potential customers are likely to visit (such as your local Chamber of Commerce website).

But don't skip print advertising altogether.

If your local newspaper is well read in the community, advertise weekly in the classifieds under homes for sale and/or in the real estate section. If photos of your homes appear muddy in the newspaper ads,

try getting a pen and ink sketch of a property. It will appear much more legible, crisp, and elegant. Plus, it will position you as an innovative marketer. Also place "institutional" ads about yourself and/or your agency that include your photo and qualifications, as well as testimonials from clients. Show your website address in large letters to direct readers to your site where they can see many photographs of each of your listings and learn more about you.

Take advantage of other forms of print advertising such as:

- Local real estate magazines—whatever is popular in your area. These magazines are often picked up by tourists (and locals) looking for a home.

- Postcard mailings. Most of your homes will be sold locally. Postcards are an efficient way to reach out to targeted areas in your market.

- Your personal brochure. You will want to have a personal brochure about you and your company to have on hand at open houses and to send out to new prospects. Be sure to bring your personal brochure to networking events as well.

It's true that most home sales now originate on the Internet. But don't ignore the clients who enjoy reading the newspaper or leafing through a brochure.

Use a professional photographer.

PHOTOGRAPHY IS KEY to any real estate business. Photographs are the primary lure to encourage a buyer to preview a property.

Great photographs draw people in, but poor photographs will turn people away. Hire a professional photographer to take beautiful images that will create a powerful story for marketing a home.

A professional photographer knows how to capture an image utilizing the best light. Allow your photographer to choose the time of day to photograph the property.

A single room may require multiple photographs to capture all it has to offer. For example, an exquisite living room could boast beautiful beamed ceilings, dramatic windows, sparkling hardwood floors, and a wood-burning fireplace. A series of photos to highlight each feature could show the room to its best advantage.

Photographers know how to tell a story through pictures, and that's exactly what you want to do with the photographs of homes you list. Capture vignettes that inspire buyers. Strike a balance between photos that show the entire room as well as details like sconces, moldings, or architectural elements. Small details can really make a difference when clients are choosing a home.

I cannot emphasize enough the importance of partnering with a professional photographer to showcase your listings no matter the price point. It simply isn't a step any real estate agent should skip. This goes for all listings, $200,000 to $5,000,000+. Guaranteed, your listings will stand out from all the rest!

Try a sketch.

PHOTOGRAPHY IS THE best way to showcase your listing on a website and online. But you will want to order a pen and ink drawing of your listing in order to pre-market the home before the garden has been spruced up and exterior painted.

Consider hiring a sketch artist to do a professional rendering of your listing. A sketch will bring cachet to all of your listings. (I do this for every listing no matter the price point—all clients deserve the best!) Why not position yourself as the agent who represents each client with platinum service rather than the agent who breaks her clientele into categories from bronze to gold? Give 110 percent to each and every client!

If you are selling condos in a project not yet built,

or if you are working with a builder who builds custom homes, a rendering of the finished home is key. A sketch is an excellent way to market a property long before it has been completed. It's easy for the illustrator to provide a detailed rendering of a property not yet finished. An illustrator is able to "embellish" the bushes and trees before they are pruned or planted and disregard the cracks in the walls of the home!

Often a photograph does not replicate well in the newspaper, but a sketch will look crisp and clear.

A professional rendering can be used not only in advertising, but also given as a gift to the buyer—printed on notecards, it's the perfect way for them to announce their new home, or framed and hung on their wall, it's a memento the buyer will keep forever.

Send postcards.

ONE OF THE most effective advertising campaigns a real estate agent can use is sending oversized post-cards. These 5-1/2 x 8-1/2" cards (half the size of a sheet of paper) are mini-billboards in your clients' mailbox.

Postcards are visual—they jump out at you. Like a billboard, you immediately grasp the point of a well-designed postcard. It's more effective to show a home than to write long paragraphs about it.

Postcards are not immediately discarded the way a letter can be. Most people will read what's on a postcard because it doesn't need to be opened. It's right there.

You can target your audience for a postcard mailing. Decide which location you would like to serve and the price range of a home you feel most comfortable selling. Then send postcards to your targeted audience.

Here's a way to start with postcards: budget for six months of oversized postcards—500 per month at $1 each (your actual price may vary). That's a $3,000 budget.

Have a professional image of the property you want to sell on the postcard. Also be sure to include your name and contact information along with your photograph. You won't have much room, but include a brief description about the home, and if you are organized, make this an announcement inviting the neighbors to your Sunday Open House. These kinds of postcards will not only help you sell properties, they can generate leads for future listings.

There are many resources on the Internet that will help you construct and mail a postcard or oversize postcard mailing. Work with your local title company to pick out the demographics of the clients you are trying to reach.

Keep your branding the same in each mailing. Your real estate company will have its own branding and a printing company to use. Use what the company offers—it's likely to be at a good price and look professional.

The good old-fashioned postcard is still a great way to reach a specific audience with your message. Remember, not everyone is on the Internet—like my mom!

Treat luxury properties differently.

"Let me tell you about the very rich.
They are different from you and me."
—*F. Scott Fitzgerald, "The Rich Boy," 1926*

WHEN A SELLER is listing a home worth a lot of money (think seven figures), it's likely there will be more to market: more glamour, more bells and whistles, more to photograph, more details. You now have a golden opportunity to market an incredible home, so take advantage of it. Don't miss the boat!

Why not host an evening preview party at the property for neighbors and clients, and a "twilight tour" for real estate agents? Parties are a wonderful way to showcase a property and meet potential clients. Have a professional photographer at the event to give you fodder for future blogs and social media postings.

When you have a luxury property, hire a professional to shoot a video about the home. You can use the video on YouTube. And don't stop there. Add the video to your website, and scatter it throughout your various social media platforms. I continually use my luxury video from years ago in my marketing presentations as needed, and of course it sits on YouTube, my LinkedIn page, and more. Put together a special brochure about the property. You may want to hire a public relations firm to drum up media coverage. It's likely the local paper will carry an article about a prestigious property for sale, especially if you advertise the property heavily. A special mailing to homeowners who have similar luxury homes in the neighborhood is a must.

If you want to take on a luxury listing, be prepared to spend money on marketing in order to sell the home and make a splash in the meantime. Don't make the mistake of thinking that the gorgeous property will sell itself. It won't!

To skimp on marketing a luxury home is tantamount to quitting just before the finish line. An agent who goes the extra mile by utilizing all the tools in his or her arsenal will satisfy clients and sell more homes.

Write a love letter.

I'VE SEEN THIS technique work for buyers and sellers alike.

You may think that a real estate transaction is a cold-blooded business affair, but it's not. Quite the contrary, emotions run high.

When a buyer or seller conveys real emotion about a home, a transaction that was going nowhere can suddenly take a turn for the better. Sometimes it happens when the would-be buyer writes a love letter about the home. It might begin:

Dear Bianca and Chase,

My family and I truly fell in love with your home the very moment we stepped over the threshold. We just knew it had to be ours . . .

The letter should be heartfelt. When it expresses a true sentiment, it can make the difference between a sale or a rejection. Sellers want to know who will be buying their home, and they want to be sure the home will be loved and cared for. One time, my husband made a deal for a buyer for $100,000 less than the highest offer. It was the buyer's letter and my husband's glowing presentation that sealed the deal!

A seller can also write a love letter about her own home. She can mention all the fabulous times they had in their home, talk about their terrific neighbors, and the town's excellent schools. A nicely written love letter can do wonders to turn a skeptical buyer into a gung-ho buyer.

People connect with a home. It's the place they live with their family, a place where they seek comfort, build memories, and entertain friends and relatives. A letter about a home that comes from the heart can be one reason why a home sells.

Real emotions count in real estate.

Tell the seller to take a hike.

WHEN YOU ARE showing a home, make sure the seller is not home.

Buyers can be much more candid about what they like (or dislike) about a home when the seller is absent. They may be reluctant to express their true feelings when the seller is lurking about. Buyers feel like they are intruding in the seller's home and do not stay as long as they would if the seller weren't around.

There are too many things that can go wrong when a seller hangs around during a showing.

One time my seller popped in during an inspection and the buyer happened to mention the oven wasn't working. The seller nonchalantly said she would have it repaired. In the end, this seemingly small gesture turned into an expensive nightmare when the part wasn't available.

I worked with one seller who had a home full of exquisite antiques. She was so anxious to sell the home she promised the buyer that she would part with furnishings worth tens of thousands of dollars. She had second thoughts later, but it was too late. The furniture became part of the deal, much to the regret of the seller (and her family). Note: Before showing a home, have the seller remove any fixtures she wants to take with her, or you risk creating significant issues that may result in a lost sale and perhaps a lawsuit. Real estate agents are not in the furniture business!

A seller might also say something like, "The roof is perfect," when, in fact, there are problems with the roof. An inspection later may disclose some issues about the roof that the buyer thought was in good shape, creating mistrust. The buyer may begin to question other things the seller said or disclosed in writing.

Keep the seller and buyer apart until after the closing!

PART THREE

Working with Clients

Be the captain of the ship.

THINK ABOUT TRAVELING on a ship. The captain knows where the ship is going. The captain gives orders and disseminates information from the top so everyone knows what's going on and what needs to be done.

To sell a home successfully, you need one leader, one single point of contact—one captain. That captain is you, the real estate agent.

As captain, it should be made clear to all parties that you are in charge. Communication for all parts of the transaction should come through you. That shouldn't be too hard, especially for e-mailed communiqués. But you'll have to keep your antennae out to make sure you are in the loop at all times: I once had a lender tell a client it was okay for the client to book the movers on a certain day. As it turned out, that day wasn't practical because of complications with the transaction. And as it turned out, the complications were the fault of that very lender! Had the lender been communicating with the captain (me), I would have been able to inform all parties, thereby avoiding disappointment. I only learned about it after the fact. A situation such as this could easily have been avoided.

Make sure everyone in a transaction knows that all decisions involving the sale of the home must flow through you. As captain, the ultimate responsibility lies with you. It's your job and it is the only way to be sure all parties are doing what they should.

Fill out your real estate checklist.

REAL ESTATE IS a business filled with details. There are timetables and deadlines to be met, appointments to travel to, meetings to schedule with a large cast of characters. And keeping all the details straight is part of your job. Most agents don't have a lot of support staff to help keep them organized.

I advise keeping two checklists for all of your listings: a "transaction checklist" and a "seller's progress checklist." *Realtor Magazine* has sample lists that you can obtain online. Here are the main features of each list:

The Transaction Checklist

This list is for the basics of the transaction and includes essential items such as the property address and MLS number. It also includes contact information

for all the parties involved in the transaction, including the buyer, seller, and attorneys, if applicable. The Transaction Checklist will also include contact information for the title/escrow company, mortgage lender, appraiser, and home inspector, plus other suppliers such as the termite inspector and contractors who may be making repairs to the property. You'll find yourself referring to this list time and time again throughout the entire transaction.

The Seller's Progress Checklist or Escrow Information Sheet

This list will help you prepare for the closing on the property. It includes an updated preliminary title report, mortgage details for payoff, utility information, and permits and repairs that have been completed. It will also detail information about transfer taxes, the settlement sheet, contingency periods, and, of course, the closing date. (Note: the items on this checklist will vary from region to region, based on the laws and ordinances in your area.)

By keeping these sheets for every property you list or sell, you will be able to access the information you need on a moment's notice.

So be like Santa Claus. Keep your lists. And check them twice.

Be like Jeeves.

IN THE HILARIOUS stories by P. G. Wodehouse, the butler Jeeves is always around to rescue his employer Bertie Wooster from the misadventures he gets himself into. Jeeves makes a special concoction when Bertie's had too much to drink the night before—and he knows without asking when Bertie needs one.

As a real estate agent, you are in charge of all the details—every last one.

Be with your clients while they are reviewing and filling out the transfer disclosure statements. It's crucial that clients report what they know and detail work they have done recently and in the past on their home, no matter how small, in order to alleviate any potential risk of not disclosing everything they know about their home. Ask them about the details so they don't forget anything.

It is crucial to attend all seller pre-inspections and all buyer inspections. Listen to what the inspector is saying. Most buyers and sellers have a hard time understanding the information and it is up to you to help them put it into perspective. You can explain their options and reiterate the inspection information more simply. Remember, you do this every day and you are intimately familiar with the terms used. Buyers and sellers are probably looking at the inspector sideways and asking, "What does that mean? Is that horrific?"

Pay attention at closing. Loan documents can be complicated and may be inaccurate. Questions will be answered and explained by the title officer, but you should be present for moral support and to make sure your client understands everything fully. Sometimes you will need to step in and ask a question on your client's behalf.

You are the professional hired to do a job, so do it well, from beginning to end, or (should I say) closing!

Convince sellers to reject being a FSBO (For Sale by Owner).

YOU WILL RUN into homeowners who tell you they are considering working with you but also thinking about selling their home themselves. There is an old saying that someone who is her own lawyer has a fool for a client. The same idea applies to real estate. Try to convince a seller that going it alone is a big mistake.

"For Sale by Owner," aka FSBO, can seem attractive to a seller. There is no real estate commission (on the listing side) to pay! But we usually get what we pay for. So much can go awry in a real estate transaction that hiring a professional real estate agent is a smart investment.

Without a real estate professional as a guide, a seller will often price the home incorrectly or emotionally—either too high or too low. Then the home may sit and not sell, or may undersell. FSBOs may not be aware of new ordinances and laws, or of the idiosyncrasies of the area that an agent can turn to the seller's advantage. And without a good working knowledge and relationships with all of the various parties, including agents, service providers, and appraisers, a FSBO can easily end up in a very difficult transaction or, even worse, a lawsuit.

A FSBO doesn't have access to required contracts, disclosures, and other paperwork. If certain documentation is overlooked, FSBOs risk legal action.

A FSBO typically will not have strong working relationships with local service providers such as appraisers and contractors, or the expertise required to understand their reports. A real estate agent who represents, guides, and supports a seller can protect him from unscrupulous service providers.

Educate your sellers on the dangers of establishing themselves as a "For Sale by Owner." You might even want to share your views in a newspaper article, in an ad, or on your own website or blog. Stand up for your profession!

RULE

29

Don't rely on online services for pricing.

ONE BLUNDER THAT too many home sellers (and some newly licensed real estate agents) make is relying on online services such as Zillow to set the listing price of the home. Professional real estate agents have more knowledge than these online services.

Here's why: the online services deal in data analysis. But data doesn't always account for less tangible factors. When there are no sales on a particular street for several months or more, or where the cost of housing repairs is high for one home and much less for another similar home, or where a first-floor condo is competing with a fifth-floor condo, the online

DEBBI DiMAGGIO

67

services can be very misleading. In the past, I noticed Zillow didn't take into consideration the difference between two towns that share a zip code. One town has an exceptional school district and its own police and fire departments, and the other lacked those features and could not even come close to comparing.

Other differences the online services don't catch: homes with multiple stairs before accessing the front door versus a level-in entry; whether or not the bathrooms and kitchens are updated; the condition of a home, including its foundation, electrical system, or water heater; homes with no garage, a one-car garage, or more; and the curb appeal of the home. A computer program simply cannot factor in all of these items. Those little extras can account for hundreds of thousands of dollars.

Establishing value from an online real estate service is like getting medical advice from a website. Sometimes it can shed some light on your question. But more than likely, you will need to see a specialist.

Be conservative when pricing a home.

HERE'S A TYPICAL scenario: Clients want to sell their home in a well-established neighborhood. You generate a market evaluation and come up with a reasonable selling price of, say, $900,000. The clients tell you, "We need to get at least $1,000,000 for the home, so we want to list our home higher." What do you do? Here are a couple of options:

One: You could take the listing at the higher price. After all, if you refuse to list the home, you can bet somebody else will. If the home doesn't sell, you can probably convince the sellers to lower the price later.

But that may be faulty reasoning. If you go along with the higher price, you'll probably end up with disappointed sellers. And if they suddenly lower their price substantially, you may be chasing the market down. Their home is now old news. The best time to sell a home is within a week to ten days after it is listed. There's an excitement about a new home on the market. Everybody wants to see the new inventory, and someone (or perhaps several people) visiting the home may actually bid on it right away—if the seller is ready to accept offers.

Two: You can attempt to convince the sellers to list the home at a price closer to the market value. Explain that listing the home closer to what you have established as the market value will generate more showings and typically more offers. If the sellers do list the home below market value, the market will usually take care of it. That's when the seller may receive multiple bids, commonly referred to as a "bidding war." Of course, an agent doesn't have a crystal ball and can never make promises. Use data and facts to establish a market value.

You may be taking a risk by trying to convince a seller to list at a lower price. They may decide not to list with you. But sometimes it makes sense to walk away from a listing opportunity if you do not think the value they want to market their home at is accurate. These sellers may even come back to you when they see that they cannot sell their home at their chosen price.

It's important to let your potential clients know that buyers do not care what the seller wants for their home, or what they spent on their improvements. If you price the property accurately, a seller will have the best opportunity to find a buyer—and maybe multiple offers!

Stay firm on your commission.

COMMISSION RATES VARY. Most real estate agents charge between five and six percent, and the commission can be ten percent or higher for vacant land.

Sellers want to pay the lowest commission possible, and some will try to negotiate with you on your commission rate.

In most cases, you should stay firm. Occasionally there will be a must-have property that you or your agency really wants, and you will have to negotiate a lower fee. But that should be the rare exception. For most transactions, you will want to stay firm.

Explain to clients who ask for a reduced commission why you have set the commission rate you have established. Agents do not receive the total amount of the commission. The commission is split with the buyer's agent. A part of your commission goes to your firm. The top-line number is not what your share of the commission will be.

It's fair to remind clients that if the deal does not go through, you do not receive a penny. Agents can invest hard work, money, and time for months trying to market a home that does not sell. The neighborhood might not be as desirable, the home may have some structural issues, the seller may not be realistic in terms of list price or cooperate by making the necessary improvements to best market the home.

Besides all your time spent on marketing a property, you and your firm will spend real dollars advertising the home. Those dollars will be spent whether or not the home sells. In many ways, taking on a home sale is like a lawyer taking a case for a share of the monetary recovery. And lawyers charge 33 percent of the recovery for their time!

For any number of reasons, sometimes a home simply does not sell, and despite all of an agent's efforts, he or she won't earn a cent for all that work and time invested. That's a risk you take with every client, and it's part of the reason why you should stand firm on collecting the full commission when a property does sell.

If a client balks at paying your commission or threatens a "for sale by owner" approach or listing with another agent, you might want to walk away. Some clients can never be satisfied. Trust your intuition!

Don't take it personally.

FOR MANY OF your clients, selling or buying a home will be the largest financial transaction in their lives. Their emotions will often be on edge, and it's up to you to be the adult in the room.

Put yourself in your clients' shoes. Buyers are making a huge commitment and are never sure it is the right move. The new home may be a bit too much for them financially. Repairs may need to be made. They are starting to suffer buyers' remorse. They might be going through a divorce or borrowing money from a relative. Have patience!

It is even tougher on sellers. They want out of their current home. They may have signed a deal on another home. They're worried that the whole deal could go south at any minute. They think the buyers will get cold feet, or want more money to fix a leaky roof, or that there will be a last minute hitch in the buyers' loan.

I was touring a husband and wife in the Oakland Hills. The family was considering relocating from Florida. The home they owned in Florida was much larger than what the same dollars could buy in the San Francisco Bay Area. I can still hear that woman shrieking to her husband, "I am *not* going to live in that! I come from a huge home with *gates* and I live like a *princess!*" Whenever I see the gates in the opening of *The Real Housewives of Orange County* reality TV show, I remember my Florida princess. Needless to say, they did not take the job or make the move.

It often seems our clients are taking their fears and frustrations out on us. What to do . . . pause and count to ten. Take a breath, and then respond professionally, with confidence and reassurance. As Michael Corleone said in *The Godfather*, "It's not personal, it's strictly business."

Pre-prepare an offer.

PRESENTING AN OFFER is one of the most crucial events in the life of a real estate agent. Make sure everyone's ducks are in a row before you make an offer on behalf of your buyer.

First of all, be sure the buyer really can go ahead with the purchase. I refer all my buyers to a local lender or mortgage broker who has a proven track record of getting deals done. When a buyer works with me, I insist that the buyer is pre-approved and we are all clear about what they can afford to purchase. If your buyer is not pre-approved, refer him to a qualified lender so the buyer can get approved for a mortgage. It doesn't take long at all— typically a buyer can be approved verbally in a few days and in writing in seven days or less if needed. However, the buyer must fill out the application and provide all documentation requested by the lender or mortgage broker.

Another trend is to perform a pre-inspection before presenting an offer. It will cost the buyer $500 to $800 to have a home inspected, and some buyers may be reluctant to spend the money even before they win the bid. But when you can come in with an offer that does not have a home inspection contingency, the seller will feel more comfortable with your offer. In a seller's market, it is not unusual for a buyer to present a non-contingent offer, which includes: an over-the-asking-price offer, no loan contingency, no appraisal contingency, and no home inspection contingency— and typically includes a 21- to 30-day close or less.

By getting rid of potential problems and roadblocks ahead of your offer presentation, you can entice a seller to favor your bid over competitors. The more problems and unknowns you clear up prior to presenting your offer, the more likely the seller will sign your contract!

Put the right offer on the table.

BUYERS WANT A bargain. Depending on the market, buyers will have different expectations. In some markets, a buyer will assume that the listing price is just the start of a conversation. A buyer may think, "I'll offer less because they are expecting to negotiate." In a seller's market, a buyer will understand that the list price is an invitation to make an offer and the selling price will actually be much higher than the asking price.

Either way, there are many considerations the buyer may not be aware of. And it is your job as a real estate agent to set the buyer straight.

In a hot market, a buyer may not get a second bite at the apple. The home may go in a flash. Buyers have said to me, "I could have paid that." In that type of market, I tell my clients to make their first offer a great offer. If you really want the home, now is your opportunity to grab it. A hot market doesn't present many opportunities for buyers, so you must educate your buyer from the beginning that they should not try to negotiate price if they love a home. It usually takes buyers two failed attempts before they prevail—three's a charm!

Even if the market is not especially hot, I counsel my would-be buyers to make a good offer, not too far below the price, where they would be happy to buy the home. If the initial offer is too low, even in a slow market, the seller may be disappointed—even insulted—and not make a counteroffer.

There are some situations where a low offer does make sense. I understand that in some communities around the country, homes are listed far higher than the price they reasonably expect to get. This tactic doesn't usually work and can backfire. Time will be lost and the price will inevitably come down. But if you find yourself in that type of community, an offer 20 or 30 percent below the asking price might be quite reasonable. Similarly, in a foreclosure situation or when a home has been languishing for months or even years on the market, the asking price may have no relation to the value of a home. It is up to you as the real estate agent to assess the accurate market value to help your client make a reasonable bid.

Your job is to help the buyer make a Goldilocks offer. Not too hot. Not too cold. Just right.

Close the deal.

IT ALL HAPPENS at the real estate closing. A check is exchanged for a deed and a key. Hands are shaken and all's well that ends well.

As a real estate agent, your job is to make sure the closing goes as smoothly as possible.

I've learned how to make sure the deal actually closes. Here are a few tips:

- Be sure the buyer makes a final walk-through of the property. In a fast-paced market where quick closes are the norm, a buyer may not find the time to return prior to close, especially with some 14-day closes!

- Make sure all the mortgage paperwork is done on time and done correctly. Keep on top of the appraiser, the lender, the title company, the lawyer, and anyone else involved in the closing. It's your job to manage the entire real estate process from beginning to end. An incorrect rate or omitted fee, for example, can put the entire closing into a state of panic and delay the close.

- Check the settlement statement ahead of time. Make sure all the charges are entered correctly for your client, whether buyer or seller.

- Coordinate with all the necessary parties to be sure everyone who needs to be there is at the closing. This varies from state to state. In California it may include just the buyer and her agent or the seller and her agent. But in New York, this may include an attorney, both agents, and both buyer(s) and seller(s). If it is typical in your area, you might have a representative from the mortgage company present, just in case.

Communication with all the parties involved in a closing is a must. Closings by their very name should be final. Make sure you have everything in place to make your closings successful. *FINI!* (That's Italian for final!)

Be on time.

NO. DON'T BE on time. Be five minutes early.

Many of your appointments are to show a home. These showings are like a performance. You want to be at the site a little ahead of time so you can compose yourself and get ready for the big show. If you arrive even a few minutes late, you risk being met by an angry buyer. You'll be in a negative situation from the get-go, and you might not be able to overcome your initial impression.

Sometimes an emergency crops up or a previous appointment takes too long. Text to let them know. Stuff happens.

Prepare for that eventuality by spacing your showings further apart. Showing a home sometimes takes much longer than you planned for. Give yourself a little breathing room. If you are running late, contact the person you are meeting. Give him an estimate of what time you'll be showing up. It's the polite thing to do.

Being harried does not have to be an occupational hazard of being a real estate agent. When you manage your calendar and schedule well, you'll look organized and professional. And just as in preparing a home for market and presenting it well, you as a real estate agent get one chance to make a good first impression.

PART FOUR

Building Your Business

Form your dream team.

REMEMBER THE ORIGINAL dream team? It was the 1992 United States men's Olympic basketball team. Even if you are not a sports nut, you will probably recognize some of the names from that team: Michael Jordan, Larry Bird, Patrick Ewing, and Magic Johnson, to name a few. The team was so dominant that its worst performance in the Olympics was a 32-point victory. No game was close. No gold medal was easier.

If you want to succeed as a real estate agent, you should put together your own dream team. You're the head coach, and you are going to select the players.

Start with a title company and/or lawyer who you know will do a great job for your clients. Work with people who are responsive to your questions—people you can contact at a moment's notice. Real estate never sleeps, especially when there is an issue that must be solved before a sale is made or a closing takes place.

Fill out your roster with appraisers, inspectors, and contractors you trust. You want to partner with professionals who come in with fair estimates and finish their jobs on budget and on time. You want quality work performed by service providers you can rely on.

Don't forget the star of your team: your client. Be sure to educate your clients on the importance of pre-market preparation and make sure clients work with you to do everything possible to position their home for a successful sale. Your clients are the key to your success, and you may have to turn down a potential client who may not have the same vision for mutual success. Trust your intuition. You will know when a potential client is not a good fit.

Put together your own dream team and go for the real estate "gold"!

Avoid the four biggest mistakes new agents make.

SO YOU'RE ABOUT to start work as a brand-new real estate agent! Congratulations!

I'm here to set you on a strong footing. Let's start by learning the four biggest mistakes new agents make:

1 **They think that they are employees.** Real estate agents are almost always independent contractors. They may work with a brokerage, but their compensation is normally commission, not salary. Therefore, real estate agents are entrepreneurs. Each agent operates his or her own business, so a business plan is a must.

2 **They don't have enough funding.** As an independent contractor, a real estate agent

cannot count on a salary to get through the start-up phase. Even with listings right away (which is highly doubtful) and an immediate sales success or two, it will take a while before the closings take place and the money rolls in. New agents should have at least three months' worth of living expenses on hand before beginning the job. Six months' worth of living expenses is even better. New agents must spend money to market themselves, and if they are lucky enough to have a listing, will need the funds to market that home for sale. Without a reserve, new agents will quickly feel financial pressure. Working a second job might be a necessity in the early months, unless there is another means of financial support during this transition.

3   **They neglect their education.** There is a lot to learn about real estate and becoming a great agent. Much of this will be learned over time. But new agents should spend as much time as possible educating themselves. There are free and paid courses that will enhance professional development. There are plenty of books and videos that will help you become a better professional. There is a great deal of information available on the Internet. Brokerage companies will also have their own training classes and programs. Take advantage of every education opportunity available. And the best source of learning will be hanging out in the office with fellow agents. Listen to how they

speak with their clients and what they say. Ask questions. Ask a fellow agent or broker if you can tag along on an inspection or listing appointment. Shadowing a successful agent is by far the best way to gain accurate knowledge about your specific market. Look, listen, and learn.

4   **They don't have a marketing plan.** Even with a business plan for the first year, a new agent needs a marketing plan as well. After weeks of consultation and observation of how other agents handle marketing, a new agent should establish a plan for marketing herself and create a budget.

Choose the right real estate firm.

NEW REAL ESTATE agents (and even experienced agents) often make a simple mistake that will keep them from rising in the field and maximizing their income: they choose the brokerage that gives them the highest commission split.

If you go for the extra five percent or even ten percent, you may be making a huge mistake. Think about it. Would you rather work for a second-rate real estate firm with a poor reputation that doesn't offer training or support, but gives you a 90 percent split—or for a firm with a stellar reputation, excellent marketing, where all agents work as a team, where you earn 70 percent? Being short-term greedy may result in long-term failure. A hundred percent of nothing is still nothing. Don't fall into that trap.

Consider the personalities of the owners and managers of a new firm: are they looking to take all the best prospects themselves, or do they want all their agents to succeed? Do they train and support their agents? Are they readily available to answer questions? It won't take a lot of research to find out which real estate firms in town have owners who work hard to make sure their agents achieve success. Just ask around.

Consider the personalities of the other agents in the firm. Do you want a working environment where there are a lot of petty jealousies and backstabbing? Of course not. Make sure you check out the reputations of the people you will be working with day-to-day. Teamwork is important and makes for a much more pleasant and successful business environment.

Beware of extra charges to agents. Some agencies offer high commission splits but charge for everyday expenses like copies, phone services, office help, technical support, advertising costs, etc. Make sure you know all the costs involved before you sign on with an agency.

Choose wisely before making your decision. Which team do you want to align yourself with?

Learn how to negotiate.

A GREAT AGENT is a great negotiator. If you think it's not your strong suit, it's time for you to improve. There are some basic negotiating skills that everyone can learn.

- **Creativity**—A little flexibility might just get the deal done. We had a deal that wasn't going to close on time, so we worked out a rental agreement prior to close of escrow; the seller received a daily rent until the buyer was able to close. This can be risky; you'll want to be confident that the buyer is on track to close the escrow and all parties are in agreement. Be sure you have the correct paperwork in place. The form we use:

"Buyer to Occupy Property Prior to Close of Escrow."

On the flip side, if a seller needs more time after the close of escrow due to timing on their next home or other circumstances, the buyer could be flexible and willing to offer a leaseback or a free "leaseback" to the seller (common in a seller's market). Both parties sign the appropriate form detailing the lease-back terms: "Seller to Occupy After Close of Escrow."

Don't lose a deal because some of the conditions aren't perfect. Utilizing your creativity will often set the negotiations back on track.

- **Cooperation**—Try to come up with a solution that works for all parties. Don't just think about your client. If you're representing a seller, for example, don't just consider the purchase price. Maybe the buyer wants an earlier or later closing date and your seller is willing to make that accommodation. Maybe there is some work that needs to be done that you can accomplish before the closing or give the buyer a credit towards the purchase price, if justified.

  Think about how you can turn a negotiation into a win-win situation.

- **Advance knowledge**—Know the bottom line for what your client will take or offer for a home. That gives you the flexibility to close a deal in a competitive situation where time is of the essence. Here's an example: You have a client who is bidding on a home in a hot market. The home is listed for $1,000,000 and your client is comfortable making a bid of $950,000. Ask your client for the highest figure you can bid on the home. Let's say that number is $975,000. If the seller counters for $985,000, you can be confident in countering back at $975,000. If the seller then accepts the $975,000 offer, you have a deal without having to go back to reconfirm with your buyer. Remember, your reputation as an agent is on the line every day, so be clear about what you present.

Having advance authority gives you more flexibility in negotiating.

Learn how to be a good negotiator. Create solutions. It will set you apart from other agents and lead to many satisfied clients while earning you a stellar reputation in the communities you serve.

Specialize.

I KNOW A real estate agent who specializes in fore-closures and probate sales. They may not be the most glamorous properties, but he's done so many foreclosures and probate sales, he knows all the ropes. He knows what hurdles he has to jump through. He knows how to negotiate with banks to get the best price on a property. He knows how to get a loan on a foreclosed property and deal with probate attorneys and trustees on the sale of a property. He knows how to check and resolve title issues. He has all the right contacts. In his firm, he's the go-to guy when a fore-closed property or probate becomes available.

Because foreclosed properties and probate sales

tend to be lower in price than other properties, my friend doesn't make as much on each transaction as other agents do. And because foreclosed properties can have multiple liens and title problems, and probate sales come with their own set of issues, he has to work hard to have successful and solid closings.

But he has found a niche. He is a specialist. Agents from other companies seek him out to help with foreclosures and probate sales. He may hit more singles than home runs, but he is constantly busy. And boy, does he close a lot of sales!

Find your niche. Specialize. That may be in townhomes, condos, high-rise buildings, investment properties, mid-range homes, vacation properties, mansions, or a specific area or neighborhood. Become the expert.

Hit a "home" run.

THERE'S NO PLACE like home.

Especially on the Internet.

Every real estate agent should have his or her own personal website. That's your home on the web. It's the most important home you will sell!

Here's how to make your website attract attention and clients:

- **Branding**—The home page needs your logo, your slogan (if you have one), and a brief description about what makes you and your firm special.

- **Great photography**—You're selling real estate, so make sure you grab people with the quality of your images. Include photographs of the homes you sell and scenic views of your area.

- **You!**—Make sure your picture and your biography are prominent on your site. Clients like to know whom they are partnering with.

- **Testimonials**—When other people tell potential clients how great you are, that's far more effective than when you say it. Testimonials are a powerful selling tool.

- **Multi-listings**—Make sure your clients have an easy way to browse all the listings in your area. An easy-to-use search platform is a must.

- **Social media links**—Yes, you are active on Facebook (and if you're not, it's time to get started). Make sure clients can find you on Facebook with one easy click. Use your own name, not some random username that no one understands. If you want to be found, you must also be active on LinkedIn, Twitter, Pinterest, Instagram, and other social media platforms as they become popular. Your goal is to be found and get hired!

- **Contact information**—Provide many ways for your clients to get in touch with you: office phone, home phone, cell phone, e-mail, text. And make sure you respond ASAP when someone contacts you!

- **Tips**—Provide your clients, potential clients, and viewers with helpful information on how to buy and sell a home. Yes, give it away. People are looking for information when they search the Internet. When you are the source of great information, clients will seek you out.

- **The fine print**—In California, don't forget your CalBRE number—it's required. Whatever state you live in, there's probably some identifying information that has to be included on your home page. Do it. Never cut corners in real estate.

As you know, the first impression means everything. Make sure your website is a huge welcome mat greeting your clients. Welcome Home!

Embrace the Internet.

HERE'S A STATISTIC from a study by the National Association of Realtors® that should make you take notice. In 2014, 43 percent of buyers found the home they purchased through the Internet. Only one percent found the home through a newspaper ad.

Now, there is a place for newspaper advertising, but ... if you are not using the Internet, you are running backward. Fast.

These trends will continue. You have to be on the Internet to survive.

Part of having a presence on the Internet is embracing social media. I've spent countless hours on the Internet, on my Facebook page, looking at listings, trying out new apps.

Some of my younger clients only want to communicate via text message. Okay. I'm there.

Instagram? I'm there with pictures of my listings.

I also have a LinkedIn presence because it's important to keep up with my fellow real estate agents and connect to agents around the country (and around the world) through professional groups and conversations.

I know many agents who like the personal touch, the phone conversation, the meeting in the office.

They're right! High touch is just as important and effective as high tech. You have to engage in both.

You can't ignore the Internet or social media. It may not be your favorite way of interacting, but you have to participate. That 43 percent figure should be on your mind.

You need to hang out where your clients are. And increasingly, that's on the Internet and on social media. I personally find social media, and especially my favorite platform, Instagram, very inspiring. The world is filled with people sharing beautiful images and motivational messages. Don't miss out!

Look for leads in unlikely places.

GOOD REAL ESTATE agents are like detectives. They are constantly looking for clues for their next listing.

Look off the beaten track for leads. Here are ten ideas for finding your next listing:

1   Estate sales—When all the items in a home are being sold, often a family wants to sell the real estate as well, since it is usually the estate's largest asset.

2   Garage sales—When a family gets rid of unwanted items, it could mean they are starting to prep for a home sale.

3   Carpet cleaners—People often clean their carpets when thinking about a move.

4   Nursing homes—Sometimes patients need to sell a residence to pay for continuing care. If you know the owners of nursing homes, they may think of you when a resident needs to sell a home.

5   Title companies—They may know of properties that have title problems. With a little digging, you may find a great listing.

6   Withdrawn listings—A property that hasn't sold can be a great prospect for a new real estate agent.

7   Abandoned or vacant properties—If you are adventurous and in a strong market, consider flipping properties that can be bought cheaply and sold at a profit.

8   Model homes—Sometimes builders will sell a model home at a good price.

9   The pick-up line at your child's school— Fellow parents and teachers can be a wealth of information, and they are always asking about real estate.

10 Hotel concierges, hairdressers, estheticians— often they know the scoop!

Sniffing around doesn't always result in properties you want to list or buy. But there may be a few gems out there if you know where to look.

Plant, water, and grow your relationships.

I OFTEN MEET agents who are contemptuous of other real estate agents, even ones in their same office. I've heard, "She stole my client," and "The other agent won't let me show the home," and "That agent has no clue what the home is worth."

Don't be your own worst enemy! Don't treat other agents as competitors. In fact, other agents can be the quickest path to grow your business.

Here's why: The more you engender trust in your fellow agents, the more referrals you will receive from them. Winning a bid for your buyer and receiving referrals are the lifeblood of our business. Referrals are an ideal avenue to bring in clients, $$$$$, more clients, and more $$$$$ when your offer is accepted. Be the agent who takes on referrals and treats colleagues with kid gloves.

Here are five ways to plant, water, and grow your relationships:

1   Go out on broker or agent tours. Get to know your fellow agents. Consider yourself a colleague, not a competitor.

2   Be supportive of your fellow agents in your own company as well as in the community. A favor here, a favor there. If they ask you to help price a home, take the time to do so. Do they need someone to water the garden for a client? Yes! Sure. Why not?

3   Develop your relationships with agents outside your market. I get referrals routinely from two agents across the bridge (that's the San Francisco-Oakland Bay Bridge).

4   Be responsive when another agent calls upon you. Follow up with the referred client ASAP and keep the referring agent in the loop.

5   Pick up the phone and call other agents. Send them a handwritten thank-you note or a quick e-mail. Network with them on Twitter, Instagram, LinkedIn, and other social media sites. "Like" other agents' Facebook posts or tweets. ENGAGE!

It's easy to be nice, and you'll be surprised how much it helps your business when you develop great relationships with other real estate agents.

Learn to love floor duty.

ASK A ROOMFUL of agents what they hate about their job, and high on the list will be "floor duty." Don't agents make money by showing homes? Hanging around the office during hours of floor duty seems like a waste of time, a needless obligation imposed by the agency.

Not so fast. Learn to love floor duty.

Think of floor duty as an opportunity rather than a burden. On floor duty, you have the opportunity to catch up on paperwork, meet with clients, post comments and listings on social media, and occasionally get lucky.

I know agents who have gotten multi-million dollar listings because they were "stuck" on floor duty. You never know when a great opportunity is going to come waltzing through the door.

As the great philosopher Woody Allen once said, "Eighty percent of success in life is showing up." When you show up for floor duty, you are doing more than keeping the agency's door open. You are showing up and preparing yourself for success.

Solicit testimonials.

WHAT MAKES SOMEONE list a home with you?

Probably the biggest factor is *trust*. Trust that you will do your best to market and sell the home as if it were your own. Trust that you know what you're doing and that you always act professionally. Trust that you will work hard to find the right buyer and negotiate the best sale.

But how do you engender trust?

Solicit testimonials from former clients.

Ask every satisfied client for one. Tell them you want to use their testimonials in your advertising. They only have to write something short—three or four sentences is enough. I'd suggest asking a week or two after the closing so your great service is still fresh in your client's mind.

It's fine for you to tell everyone how great you are. But *much* more effective is for other people to sing your praises. Think about how often we read reviews today—whole businesses like Yelp and TripAdvisor have been created to give people the chance to review products and services.

Testimonials are your top selling tool. Use them liberally: on the home page of your website, in your print advertising, on your social media outreach.

Take pictures of your satisfied clients. Or better yet, take a video. A fifteen-second clip on YouTube featuring satisfied clients is a great selling device.

If you're a good real estate agent, you have plenty of satisfied clients. Don't be afraid to ask them to give you a testimonial when the job is done.

Set out the welcome mat.

IF YOU ARE a real estate agent, you're probably someone who really likes people. At your home, everyone's welcome as a guest. Be sure that your professional demeanor reflects that same attitude.

Start a relationship by saying "thank you." Thank potential clients for coming to you for information. Thank new clients for listing with you. Give clients a small gift when the home is sold to say, "Thank you for your business." Expressing thanks is always appreciated.

Be patient with clients' requests. Make allowances. Real estate clients are not intentionally trying to waste your time with unnecessary demands or unrealistic expectations. What may seem trivial to you can be a big deal to your clients. Try to solve your clients' problems, big and small, with a smile.

Communicate frequently with clients. Keep your clients totally informed every step of the way. Make it a habit to copy your clients on pertinent communications. Anticipate your clients' questions and give them a call first.

Show your clients how you are advertising their home. Running an ad? Send a copy to your client. Posting on social media? Make sure your client sees the post. Sending out a postcard? Send the postcard to your client in an envelope with a note about what you're doing.

A welcoming attitude toward all your clients makes for great relationships—and referrals from happy clients to your next clients!

Structure your time.

REMEMBER YOUR FIRST day of college? The beautiful campus, your new roommate, the books, the classes, and all that unscheduled time.

Well, being a real estate agent is kind of like being back at college. You have 24 hours of unscheduled time each and every day, and it's up to you to fill it up.

Some college students pass the time by skipping classes and partying all night. But sooner or later they pay the price for that behavior.

As a real estate agent, you are not an employee of the firm. You're a free agent. You can choose to attend office meetings or skip them. You can go on broker tours or go shopping. You can schedule an open house on Sunday or watch football all day. It's up to you.

No one is telling you what to do, where to go, and when to do it. The day is all yours.

So, you have to become organized. Here's what I do:

- I structure my typical day with regular office hours—at the very least, 9 to 5, five days a week. That is usually my minimum, as it is for many other successful real estate agents.

- I have a dedicated workspace at home as well as in the firm's office. Everything's in the cloud so I can access my records wherever I'm working. I use Google Drive all the time.

- I keep a detailed online calendar that I update with every appointment. I check the calendar every evening so I know what's coming up tomorrow, and every morning so I'm ready for what the day will bring.

- I suggest keeping online files (with double backups!) for each client, like my husband and partner does. Every piece of correspondence sent out should be put into those files along with any communications from vendors, buyers, sellers, attorneys, title companies, etc.

You have to create your own structure. Schedule your workdays and even make yourself schedule your time off. Put a plan in place and stick to it.

Be a busy (and smart) bee.

MY FAVORITE EXPRESSION is, "If you want something done, give it to a busy person."

Here's why: Most busy people know how to get things done. They take on a lot and they see things through. If your project is important, a busy person will make sure it's handled on time. And well.

Start getting busy. Do a little extra. Don't say you're too tired when a colleague invites you to an open house or preview party. Go. Put on your favorite outfit and get out there and rock it! Attend networking events, birthday parties, after-work events, and mixers. One key way for real estate agents to achieve success is to keep active and engage with people in many venues. Seek out like-minded people to connect with and partner with for mutual success.

But be smart. A successful busy person is one who is organized, can prioritize obligations, and fulfills everything she promises to do. It doesn't help to be busy if you end up disappointing people. Say "no" if an opportunity doesn't fit into your timeframe.

Be busy. But be smart busy.

Widen your "sphere of influence."

IT'S TIME TO make a spreadsheet.

This list is different from your contact list or Facebook friends or LinkedIn connections. This list is directly related to your business. It's a list of your "sphere of influence." These are people who can help you grow your business dramatically this year.

Here's who to include on this list:

- Your personal friends and your spouse's friends.

- Your spouse's co-workers who have met you.

- Your children's friends (or their parents, depending on your kids' ages).

- Your parents' friends (or their kids, depending on your parents' ages).

- Your neighbors.

- The people you exercise with, or play tennis with, or are in a book club with. Anyone you see in a social group in your everyday life.

- People you do business with: doctor, lawyer, dentist, accountant, hairdresser, facialist, car mechanic, contractor, etc.

- Family members.

- People you see often, such as the postal carrier, bank teller, local store owner, etc.

It may sound like a lot of work to keep this list, but it's not. Commit to adding a few names daily. I keep my list as a Google Spreadsheet in Google Drive. Then I can access it from any computer without having to lug my laptop around. When I meet someone new to add to the list, I can easily access the spreadsheet, make notes, and add contacts.

Now, what do you do with this list?

Keep in touch, naturally.

Send a holiday card. Occasionally send a listing announcement. Invite them to an open house.

Write a personal letter letting them know you'd love to do business with them.

Become Facebook friends. Send them e-mails about some of the work you do from time to time.

By taking advantage of your "sphere of influence," you are well on the way to selling success and having fun. You have to love and enjoy what you do in order to create success!

Throw a party!

EVERYONE LOVES A party.

A party will delight clients and agents, and create an atmosphere of fun and hospitality around your business. And if your parties are enjoyable, everyone will want to be on your guest list!

Getting your clients and other agents together will help you publicize your business and show people that you care about them. Have a party every six months to a year.

I've used lots of excuses to throw a party:

- **A "Mix and Mingle."** This is a business party where people (agents, colleagues, clients, friends, and service providers you work with) get together to have fun and exchange ideas. Partner with another business to co-host your Mix and Mingle. That's a win-win for your agency and the other business. I've held Mix and Mingles at an in-home theater show-room, at a high-end furniture boutique, and even a nail spa. The store reaps the benefit of potential new customers, while the agent has a beautiful venue to host and cultivate rela-tionships. A small bite and a glass of wine, throw in a goody bag, and you have a party!

- **An anniversary party**. Celebrate the anni-versary of when you started your business. It doesn't matter if you've been in business one year, three years, fifteen years, or forty years. Celebrating your anniversary is a great excuse for a party. You don't have to do this yourself. You can work with your agency to put on this party. And don't forget to send an invitation to your local newspaper editor and place an ad.

- **A holiday bash**. It doesn't have to be a Christmas party. Throw a Halloween open house or an Oktoberfest beer tasting or a St. Patrick's Day soiree! You're just looking for an excuse to have a good time, and create some goodwill and build strong business relation-ships at the same time.

Having a party is a great pick-me-up for yourself as well as your business. As Mae West said, "You only live once, but if you do it right, once is enough."

CONCLUSION

IT IS MY desire that we all succeed. I hope *Real Estate Rules!* provides insight, inspiration, and gentle reminders to propel your business to the next level. My goal is to communicate, educate, and inspire my clients, friends, and fellow real estate professionals. I wish you great success!

Reach out to me on Instagram, Facebook, Twitter, LinkedIn, and Pinterest—I look forward to engaging!